HOW TO BUILD
MODEL SHIPS

A VISUALIZED STEP-BY-STEP
GUIDE FOR BUILDERS OF ALL
TYPES OF SHIP MODELS

By WILLIAM NORDNER

MEREDITH PRESS /L L) **NEW YORK**

Library of Congress Card Catalog Number: 74-76806

Manufactured in the United States of America for Meredith Press by I. P. D. Publishing Co., Inc.

CONTENTS

1

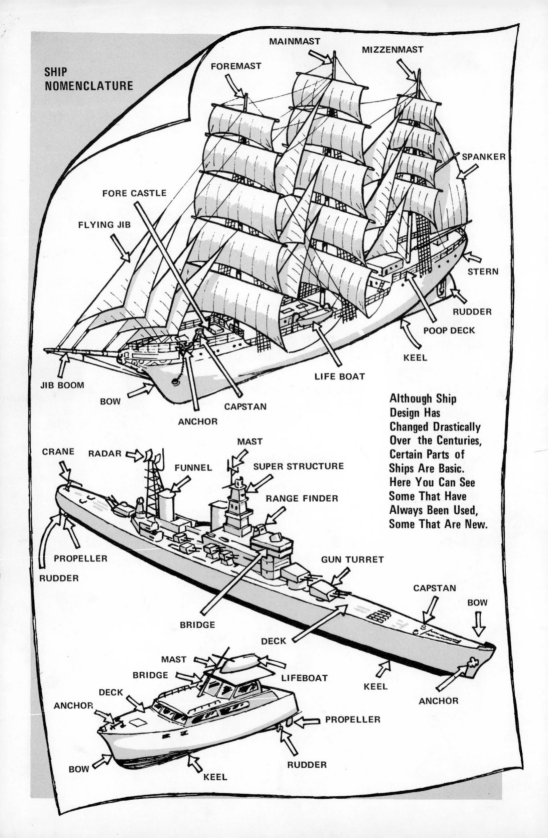

SHIP NOMENCLATURE

MAINMAST
MIZZENMAST
FOREMAST
SPANKER
FORE CASTLE
FLYING JIB
STERN
RUDDER
POOP DECK
KEEL
LIFE BOAT
JIB BOOM
BOW
CAPSTAN
ANCHOR

Although Ship Design Has Changed Drastically Over the Centuries, Certain Parts of Ships Are Basic. Here You Can See Some That Have Always Been Used, Some That Are New.

CRANE
RADAR
FUNNEL
MAST
SUPER STRUCTURE
RANGE FINDER
PROPELLER
RUDDER
GUN TURRET
CAPSTAN
BOW
BRIDGE
DECK
KEEL
ANCHOR

MAST
BRIDGE
DECK
LIFEBOAT
ANCHOR
DECK
PROPELLER
BOW
KEEL
RUDDER
ANCHOR

HOW TO BUILD MODEL SHIPS

TYPES OF SHIP MODELS AVAILABLE

	Hull Material	Type of Hull Construction	Purpose of Model
SAILING SHIPS	WOOD	SOLID	SHOW
	WOOD	PLANK ON FRAME	 SHOW
	WOOD	SOLID (Hull Carved Outside and Inside)	 WORKING
	PLASTIC	PREFABRICATED	SHOW
POWERED SHIPS	WOOD	 SOLID (Precarved Hull)	 WORKING
	WOOD	SOLID	SHOW
	WOOD	PLANK ON FRAME	WORKING
	 PLASTIC	 PREFABRICATED	WORKING
	 PLASTIC	 PREFABRICATED	SHOW

INTRODUCTION

I am attempting in this book to do something experienced model builders said was *impossible*. I have written a guidebook for beginning model builders, for recent entrants into this fascinating hobby and for those who have yet to start. So you might say this book is an introduction, beginner's guide, and refresher course to the wonderful world of model ship building.

In many ways, this era of mass production and prefabrication has actually increased the number of model builders so that today, the hobby is no longer dominated by those "purists" who make every part themselves. Now the kit hobbyists have joined the fraternity.

No one really knows exactly how many model builders there are in America—or in any other country for that matter. They number in the millions, you can be sure! Model builders of all types form clubs, enter contests, and correspond with each other all over the world. Their number is growing because there is simply no substitute on earth for the satisfaction a human being gets from being able to make something with his own hands. For a hobbyist, the admiration he receives is all the reward he needs or wants.

Perhaps the oldest and most enduringly popular branch of model building is model ship building. Perhaps it is because ships were one of the earliest of man's vehicles, and with these he conquered the seas. Perhaps it is because ships themselves have a mysterious fascination that even spacecraft cannot match. Or maybe it is because we are all sailors at heart, and the thrill our ancient ancestors felt in embarking on the full tide to conquer the angry sea, is still within us. Whatever the reason, welcome to the fascinating fraternity of model ship builders!

PATIENCE is the Secret Formula

The first thing every new model builder should do is hang a large sign near his work area that reads *PATIENCE*. Without this, you are doomed to frustration and many failures. Actually, it is a frame of mind that all successful hobbyists have developed. Often, what seems to us incredible skill is nothing more than the result of indestructible patience. In this day of automation, shrinking time and distance, young people never really have a chance to develop this trait. Take my advice—craftsmanship can be developed only through patient application. This skill requires trial and error, time and reflection. With patience and determination, anyone can develop the skill needed for successful model building.

This book will give you the fundamentals of model ship building, the basic tools you'll need, how to use them, and the time-tested techniques for fabrication and assembly. I have avoided specific models or types of ships. This is your choice, for selecting the model you wish to build is a great part of the fun. Finally, you may decide to keep this book in your hobby library always because, no matter how experienced or skilled you become in the future, the fundamentals I have gathered here will make a basic reference you will always want handy.

Good luck and have fun—that's what model ship building is all about!

CHAPTER ONE

What Kind of Model Should You Build?

If you've built a model before, you know that by the time you completed your project you were already thinking about the next. But for a newcomer, choosing his first model can be quite different, perhaps even confusing.

Before you select a model you must know what kinds are available and how difficult each one is to build. In this chapter, we will review the field and introduce you to the wide variety of basic ships and their construction.

The first question you must answer is: "Do you want to build a model that actually works, or do you want one for display only?" You will probably want to build both kinds sooner or later, but if this is your first model, we would suggest a display model. Display ("show") models are easier to build because you are concerned only with exterior detail.

Model kits are available in either plastic or wood. Wooden hulls may be either precarved, solid, or formed in the manner of real ships by fastening bulkheads to a keel, and covering that with planks.

Plastic kits are perhaps the easiest for a beginner, assuring somewhat better results for the less-skilled builder. The prefabricated plastic parts offer a high degree of detail already fashioned into them, so that the beginner is not faced with a detailing job beyond his skill. Each kit provides fairly simple instructions for assembling the parts with glue.

Many people consider a wooden model more authentic. But it's not a good idea to start on a wooden square-rigger, for instance, until you've acquired more knowledge through simpler constructions like fore-and-aft rigged sloops and schooners. Stay within your skill limits. Then, as the fascination of fitting parts together grows on you, as you gain confidence and ability, you can look forward to the pleasure of building that clipper ship, its ropes no longer a mass of confusion but a pattern of order that you understand.

Working models are those that will operate in the water. They require you to assemble moving parts that must work when your boat is launched. The simplest sailboats are, of course, propelled by a breeze. Other kits offer boats powered by gas engines or electric motors, some remote-controlled by radio.

In any case—wood or plastic, show or working—beautiful models can be built at your level of skill if you apply care and patience. Soon you will be the master of a model fleet, displaying models that you can sail or show with pride and satisfaction.

DISPLAY MODELS—Wood

Most of the finer display models are made of wood. One type of kit contains a precarved wooden hull with side rails, cabin sides, and various other pieces die-cut on sheetwood, to be separated and glued together.

Historic ships are replicas of famous vessels, past and present. Besides their beauty, their association with adventure and momentous events make them by far the most desirable show models.

On a square-rigged ship, ropes that control the yards on one mast are simply repeated on the other masts. Each rope has a name and a purpose which you can learn to identify.

Various parts and pieces are numbered to match the numbers on the building plans and instructions, making much easier a job which might otherwise seem somewhat confusing.

The rigging on single-masted sloops and two-masted schooners and yawls is naturally easier for the beginner. Kits for these are available too, including some that are for both show and operation.

Another type of display model kit uses *plank-on-frame* construction, the same method that is used to build full-size wooden vessels. Construction begins with the forming of the hull upside down.

Bulkheads, decks, superstructure, etc., are die-cut on sheetwood. Bulkheads form the frame. Planks are attached to the sides of the bulkheads to shape the hull. The boat is then turned to an upright position so that the rest of the parts (usually numbered for easy reference) can be attached to the hull.

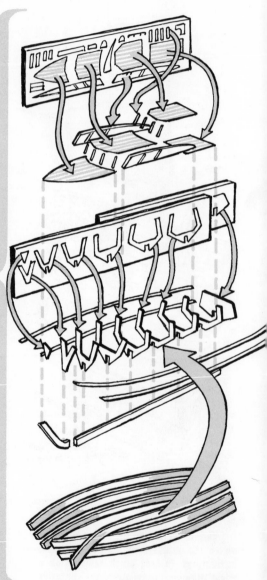

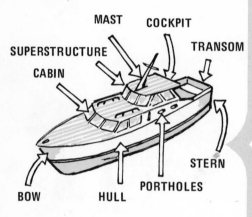

MAST
COCKPIT
TRANSOM
SUPERSTRUCTURE
CABIN
STERN
BOW
HULL
PORTHOLES

Because of its skeleton frame hull, a framed-up boat is a little lighter in weight than carved hull models. And because side planking is secured to an inner frame, accurately joined and properly glued, it is also a bit more rigid.

Plank-on-frame construction takes somewhat more work, precision, and time, but when instructions are carefully carried out, there's no reason why you can't turn out a fine boat.

DISPLAY MODELS—Plastic

Submarines have always fascinated model builders. The majority of submarine models are built for show purposes only. Operating submarine kits are also available with well-engineered fittings and accessories and using either rubberband motors or powerful miniature electric motors with dry cell battery power . . . but it takes some skill and experience to construct a sub that will submerge successfully and perform well. Most display sub kits reproduce in miniature scale and authentic detail the famous submarines of the world.

Plastic kits have completed hulls, parts, and fittings which you attach and glue into place according to instructions and plans.

One type of kit allows you to snap off one side of the hull to reveal the highly detailed interior of an atomic sub, and actually to fire missiles. These interior parts are assembled by the hobbyist who likes a challenge.

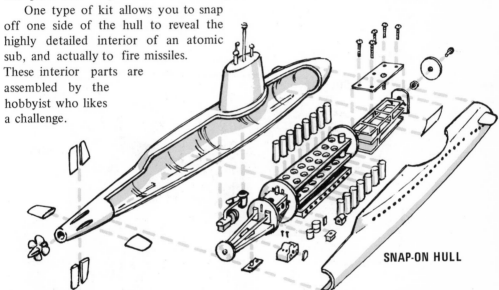

SNAP-ON HULL

All types of vessels are offered in *preformed plastic* kits: historic sailing ships with prefabricated rigging and contour sails; sturdy fighting ships copied from Navy blueprints, with flight and deck armaments; paddle steamers; ocean liners; pleasure craft; etc.

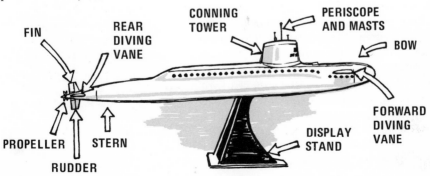

FIN

REAR DIVING VANE

CONNING TOWER

PERISCOPE AND MASTS

BOW

PROPELLER   STERN

RUDDER

DISPLAY STAND

FORWARD DIVING VANE

9

WORKING MODELS—Wood

Working models require rugged construction to withstand the gaff of rough water and handling. The better kits provide high quality balsa and hardwood parts, such as precision die-cut birch plywood frames and deck, and solid mahogany planking. Metal fittings (brass, copper, and aluminum) contribute to good workmanship. Assembly must be snug and watertight. Instruction sheets usually tell you where and how to seal the craft against leaks and seepage.

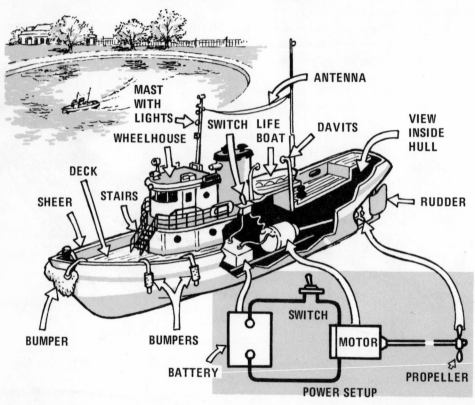

Fine working model kits supply authentic detail so that, in addition to the thrill of watching your craft dash across the water under its own power, it can be displayed and admired for its beauty and realism. Neat, precise numbers, names, and insignia are difficult for you to paint on your craft; decals do the job easily, cleanly, and efficiently.

Power for your model can be supplied by tiny but powerful gasoline engines or electric (inboard or outboard) motors, providing all the more reason for watertight compartments when an engine is enclosed in a hull. Engine and hardware may come with a kit or may be bought separately. Remote radio control adds further interest and enjoyment to operation. For real zip, you can build your own racing speedster with a hydroplane kit.

WORKING MODELS—Plastic

Some of the best of these kits are replicas copied from the original plans, paintings, and photos of the great vessels these models duplicate. Their detail will be faithful down to the smallest fittings. Some may have a few movable parts.

Since a plastic kit contains the completed hull and parts, there are no parts to be fashioned by you. They need only be cleaned of burrs, irregularities, and waste material, and then assembled and cemented watertight. When parts are not numbered, you must follow the kit's printed instructions which are keyed by number to the building plan.

CARGO SHIP

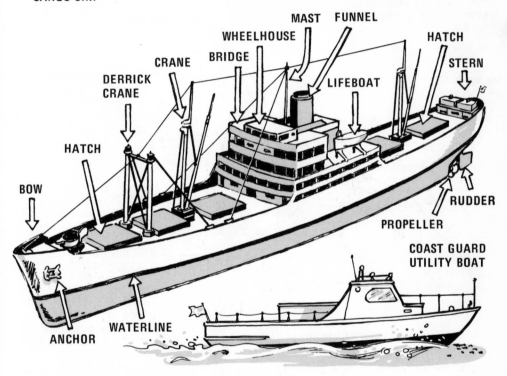

Parts are provided with holes and slots into which other parts are to be pressed. They must be joined and cemented carefully for a strong and tight job, for the finished model will be under a good deal of stress when in operation. Some parts have to be painted before assembly.

Cruisers, battleships, luxury liners, cargo ships, oilers, fishing boats, speedboats . . . here again, there is such a wide variety, each with its own fascination, that you'll find it hard to make a choice. The beginner is often tempted to choose a complicated model. Remember: start simple, and look forward to the challenge and fun of tackling more complicated models as you get surer of yourself.

WORKING MODELS—Sail

Operational sailing craft kits vary greatly in size, type, and price, from single-masted sailboats to four- and five-masted square-rigged clipper ships. A beginner's kit, low in price and easy to assemble from instructions, provides everything needed for a simple boat: prefabricated parts of balsa wood, mast, rudder, weighted keel, hemmed sails, rigging, and fittings. A more advanced kit would use a plywood frame and hull, beautiful mahogany decks and planking and metal rudder and fittings. Sailing craft built specifically for racing call for skill in both construction and seamanship.

Stability is important. Without ballast, the boat might be unbalanced and would tip over. When the keel is properly weighted with ballast the boat floats squarely upright.

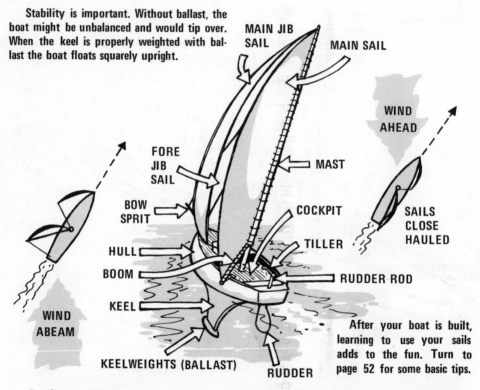

MAIN JIB SAIL

MAIN SAIL

WIND AHEAD

FORE JIB SAIL

MAST

BOW SPRIT

COCKPIT

SAILS CLOSE HAULED

TILLER

HULL

BOOM

RUDDER ROD

KEEL

WIND ABEAM

KEELWEIGHTS (BALLAST)

RUDDER

After your boat is built, learning to use your sails adds to the fun. Turn to page 52 for some basic tips.

By far the greatest art is called for in carving your own hull, shaping the parts, procuring and fitting hardware, making your own sails; that is, building and rigging a vessel from plan to finish completely on your own, somewhat in the same way full-size craft are constructed. And there is great pleasure in it, too, and great pride in watching that handiwork of yours glide majestically across the water.

Some sophisticated sailboat kits give you the option of free-sailing or radio-controlled sailing, with instructions for installing the RC (radio control) equipment. In these, the rudder is operated by remote control. In some models, radio equipment also controls the sails: raising, lowering, and tilting them to get the most out of the slightest breeze, the way big boats are handled. RC equipment is usually sold from the kit. It's a thrill but be prepared for added expense.

WORKING MODELS—Power

A speedboat kit is ideal for the novice, offering the simplest construction techniques and power installation. There is neither cabin nor superstructure nor rigging and little detail is needed. An *electric outboard motor* (with built-in "on-off-reverse" switch) runs on flashlight batteries and needs only the simplest electric wiring. The motor is merely clamped to the transom, like full-size outboards. Heavier model craft use up more current, so more voltage is supplied by *wet cells* to an *electric inboard* motor. Electric motors produce moderate speeds, far less than *internal combustion engines* can develop.

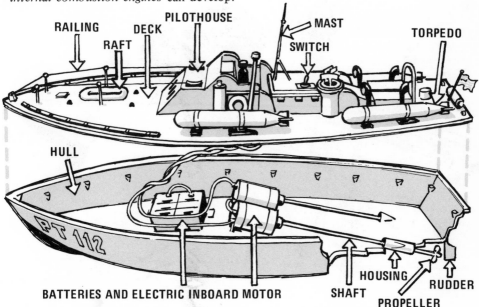

RAILING DECK PILOTHOUSE MAST TORPEDO
RAFT SWITCH

HULL

BATTERIES AND ELECTRIC INBOARD MOTOR SHAFT HOUSING RUDDER PROPELLER

Internal combustion power plants (gasoline and glow-plug engines) create more power than the electrics. Used in model craft with shallow-draft hulls, like hydroplanes, hydrofoils, airboats, etc., they can't be beat for action. Brute power, breakneck speed, screaming engine, spray, and boiling wake, all from that tiny engine! A racing boat's hull (2 to 3 feet long) must be strong enough to withstand speeds of 60 miles per hour or more. But its own speed can cause an accident and wreck it: hitting a submerged branch, riding into shore, or flipping over ripples onto its back. Wide, calm water is best for free running. In smaller shallow waters, it can be tethered to run in a circle.

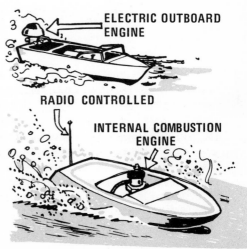

ELECTRIC OUTBOARD ENGINE

RADIO CONTROLLED

INTERNAL COMBUSTION ENGINE

CHAPTER TWO

Visualize the Model Beforehand

Hobby shops are always happy to let you look around at their merchandise and welcome your questions about various models. Just looking at the picture on the box or in the catalog isn't enough. Sometimes the picture gives the wrong idea of what a model looks like when it's finished. Before buying, open the kit and take out the hull, if no one objects; look at the masts or superstructure. These parts may give you some idea of actual size and shape—a mental image of the finished model. Satisfy yourself about the styling and overall design of the boat. If the profusion of parts dismays you, keep in mind that the instruction sheet will help to make sense of it all later. Check to see that the instructions and plans are good and clear. If you want a kit with numbered parts (a good idea for a novice), check this before you buy the kit.

Now's the time to ask yourself questions. If you're looking for a historical model or replica of an actual ship, is this one authentic? Don't forget to check to whether it's an ornamental or operating model. Would the operating model be complicated to build?

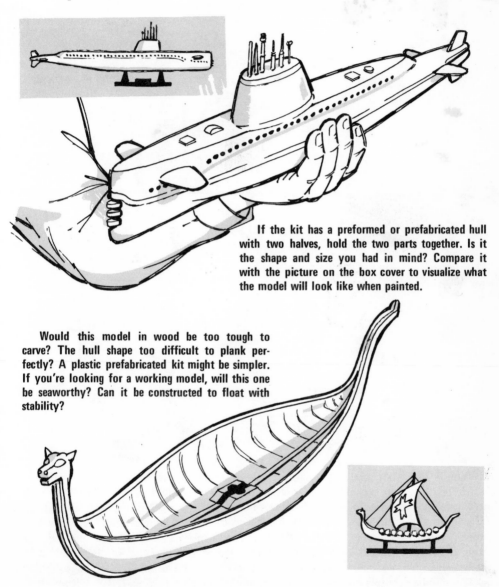

If the kit has a preformed or prefabricated hull with two halves, hold the two parts together. Is it the shape and size you had in mind? Compare it with the picture on the box cover to visualize what the model will look like when painted.

Would this model in wood be too tough to carve? The hull shape too difficult to plank perfectly? A plastic prefabricated kit might be simpler. If you're looking for a working model, will this one be seaworthy? Can it be constructed to float with stability?

If you're thinking of a powered model, do you have a place to operate it? Will you be able to set up the power plant? Will the battery compartment be watertight? If you want to install radio control someday, is the model engineered for it? Does the kit have instructions for RC installation?

How about watching some finished models in action? A good way, and an enjoyable way to clarify your thoughts on the subject, is to visit a lake or park pond where hobbyists gather to try out their craft. In many places, a town or park civic organization or local club periodically holds an official model-boat regatta.

You'll see what kind of performance you can expect from different models, which boats appear more stable, how the skippers navigate and maintain their craft, how careful they are to avoid damage. You'll see the rigging in place, the wind's effect on sails, and how sailboats hardly ever run without a "list" because the breeze "heels them over." Notice that boats with more sail have longer and heavier keels that reach deeper into the water to balance the pressure of the wind. And notice, too, that a properly designed suit of sails has a bit of slack—each bags slightly in the middle. (Display models often have sails hanging nice and flat, without the slightest looseness, because they look better to inexpert eyes.) Then, notice how a power boat stays practically on the same waterline when running at top speed. This is called "planing" the powerful motor actually tries to drive the boat up and out of the water.

As for nonoperating replicas of modern ships, some of the finest are displayed in travel agencies and shipping-line offices, and are the handiwork of professional craftsmen using complex machine tools. The best creations of amateur model-makers may be seen at model-building contests sponsored by local organizations like the Boy Scouts, Police Athletic League, or YMCA. Sometimes, competitions are run by county or state fairs or by local hobby shops. The arts and crafts or shop teacher in school may have other suggestions for you. One of the best places to pick up modeling lore is at a boat-model club where experts are always glad to share their enthusiasm and know-how with the newcomer.

See the real thing when you get the chance. Boating shows exhibit a wide variety of pleasure and sporting craft, some of which you can board and examine at close hand. And at ship piers, where liners and freighters dock and tugboats hustle, you might come upon the prototype of the very model you're interested in!

By all means, pay a visit to a nautical museum; it is worth the trip. Besides seeing the wonderful and awe-inspiring collections of old boat models, figureheads, and memorabilia, at some museums you can actually go aboard, and often down below on a great historic square-rigger or whaling schooner to look it over. Or go into an old-time ropewalk (a long covered building where ropes are manufactured), or a sail loft (where sails are cut and made), or enter other shore installations to watch them in operation.

A number of such museums and historic ships are listed on the next page.

Maritime Museums and Historic Ships

Boston Marine Society, Boston, Mass.

Cabrillo Beach Marine Museum, San Pedro, Calif.

California Museum of Science and Industry, Los Angeles, Calif.

Chesapeake Bay Maritime Museum, St. Michaels, Md.

Columbia River Maritime Museum, Astoria, Ore.

Confederate Naval Museum, Columbus, Ga.

Dossin Great Lakes Museum, Detroit, Mich.

Fairport Marine Museum, Fairport Harbor, Ohio

Flagship *Niagara*, Erie, Penn.

Fort Chambly National Historic Park, Chambly, Que.

Fort Lennox National Historic Park, Ile aux Noix, Que.

Great Lakes Historical Society Museum, Vermilion, Ohio.

H. M. S. *Nancy*, Wasaga Beach, Ont.

House of Refuge, Stuart, Fla.

Marine Museum of Upper Canada, Toronto, Ont.

Mariners Museum, Newport News, Va.

Maritime Museum, Cohasset, Mass.

Maritime Museum, Vancouver, B.C.

Maritime Museum Association of San Diego, San Diego, Calif.

Maritime Museum of British Columbia, Victoria, B.C.

Maritime Museum of Canada, Halifax, N.S.

Massachusetts Institute of Technology, Francis Russell Hart Nautical Museum, Cambridge, Mass.

Naval Aviation Museum, Pensacola, Fla.

Naval Training Center Historical Museum, San Diego, Calif.

Newfoundland Naval and Military Museum, St. John's, N.F.

Officers' Quarters Museum, Penetanguishene, Ont.

Palace Grand and S.S. Keno National Historic Parks, Dawson , Yukon

Penobscot Marine Museum, Searsport, Me.

Penticton Museum and Archives, S.S. *Sicamous*, Penticton, B.C.

Philadelphia Maritime Museum, Philadelphia, Penn.

San Francisco Maritime Museum, San Francisco, Calif.

San Francisco Maritime State Historical Monument, San Francisco, Calif.

Schooner *Lucy Evelyn*, Beach Haven, N.J.

Schooner *Wawona*, Seattle, Wash.

Seabee Museum, U.S. Navy, Port Hueneme, Calif.

Seaman's Bank for Savings, Maritime Collection, New York, N.Y.

Seamen's Church Institute of New York, Marine Museum, New York, N.Y.

Segwin Steamboat Museum, Gravenhurst, Ont.

State of North Carolina, U.S.S. *North Carolina* Battleship Memorial, Wilmington, N.C.

Steamboat *W.P. Snyder, Jr.*, Marietta, Ohio

Steamship Historical Society of America, Inc., New York, N.Y.

Submarine Library, Groton, Conn.

Suffolk County Whaling Museum of Sag Harbor, Long Island, Sag Harbor, N.Y.

Truxtun-Decatur Naval Museum, Washington, D.C.

U.S. Frigate *Constellation*, Baltimore, Md.

U.S. Frigate *Constitution*, Boston, Mass.

U.S. Naval Academy Museum, Annapolis, Md.

U.S. Naval Historical Display Center, Washington, D.C.

Whaling Museum, Nantucket, Mass.

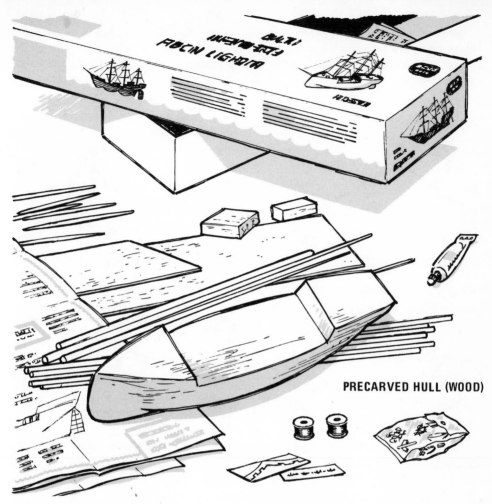

PRECARVED HULL (WOOD)

CHAPTER THREE

Lay Out the Kit Pieces

Your kit is in front of you and you're eager to start your project. But don't puncture the cement tube yet—you're not ready to start assembling, cutting, or shaping. Relax. First, you've got to know your parts and study your plans. Check to see that all parts are there, with no defects, so you won't be surprised later. Read the instructions and study the plans, now, from start to finish, so you'll be able to anticipate each succeeding step in the assembly when its time comes.

Familiarize yourself with the parts by checking them now with the plans as you read along. Sure, it takes time but it's worth it; nothing can be more frustrating than being in the middle of a delicate operation when suddenly, dripping glue tube in one hand and pieces held gingerly in the other, you discover you haven't the faintest idea what to do next.

Some plank-on-frame kits have precut parts. The boat's frame is formed by fitting numbered *bulkheads* into numbered notches in the *keel*; numbered notches in the *deck* pieces then fit onto the bulkhead's prongs. You can try fitting the parts together without cementing them, to get a preliminary feeling of the assembly process.

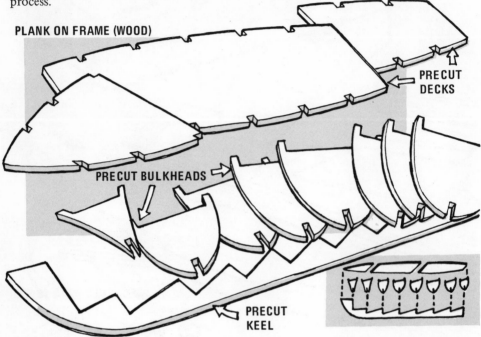

PLANK ON FRAME (WOOD)

PRECUT DECKS

PRECUT BULKHEADS

PRECUT KEEL

Another type of kit has die-cut parts that you can separate easily from the sheetwood or plywood sections on which they are printed. The long, squared *stringers*, or *chines*, will hold the frame together; then *planking* will enclose the frame, shaping the sides and bottom of the hull.

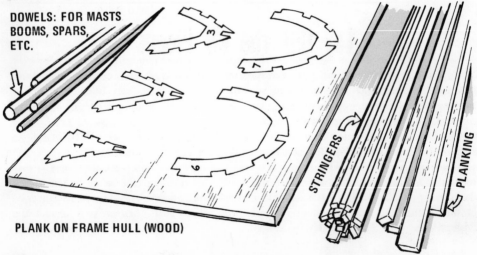

DOWELS: FOR MASTS BOOMS, SPARS, ETC.

STRINGERS

PLANKING

PLANK ON FRAME HULL (WOOD)

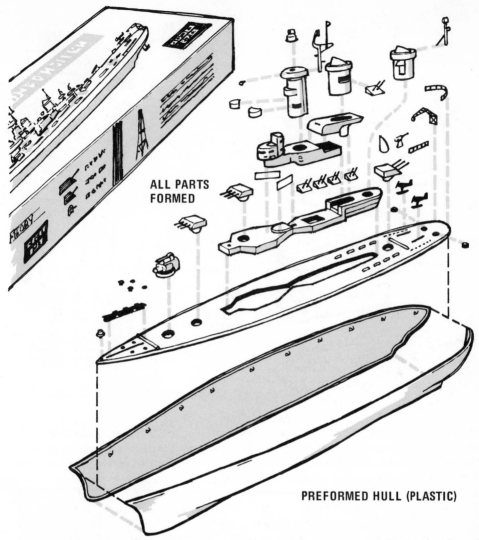

ALL PARTS FORMED

PREFORMED HULL (PLASTIC)

In plastic kits, the model parts are all prefabricated and usually have a lot of fine and authentic detail. No parts will have to be made by you. Your job will be to join and cement them as precisely as you're able, which can be an elaborate operation in the more complex kits. You will have to paint them, using the box cover painting as a guide for complete authenticity.

Check to see that all the parts are accounted for and unbroken. You can give some of the parts a trial fitting, just to get the feel of it. Become familiar with each part and its purpose *now*; guesswork could make trouble later on. The parts may not be numbered, so you'll have to refer to the pictures on the plans which show where each part and fitting is attached. Usually there are some parts that have to be painted *before* they are attached in place; note which ones they are and what kind of paint you should have ready for them.

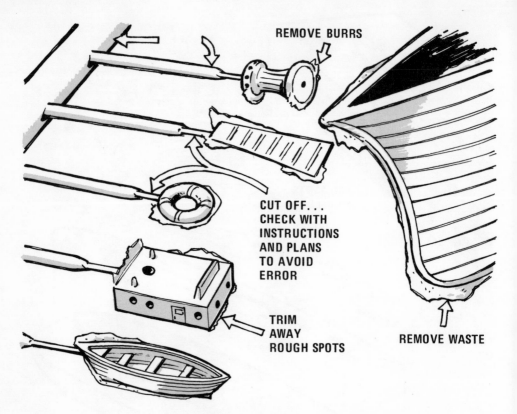

REMOVE BURRS

CUT OFF . . .
CHECK WITH
INSTRUCTIONS
AND PLANS
TO AVOID
ERROR

TRIM
AWAY
ROUGH SPOTS

REMOVE WASTE

As you separate each preformed part from the plastic tree, make sure you cut it off at the right place. Be extra careful when separating slender pieces. While you're detaching the parts, trim off burrs, rough spots, and plastic waste with a knife or razor blade. Note that some parts have pins that go into matching holes in other parts. If you have such a model, try putting the two hull halves together. Notice how the pins on one half fit into the holes in the other half. To avoid damaging a part, it's a good idea to refer to the picture before trimming or cutting to see exactly how the part should look, including any pins or tabs.

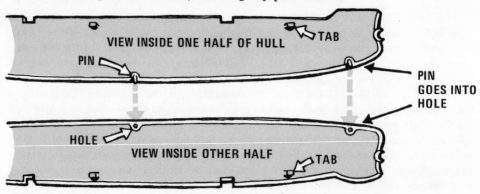

VIEW INSIDE ONE HALF OF HULL

TAB

PIN

PIN
GOES INTO
HOLE

HOLE

VIEW INSIDE OTHER HALF

TAB

The solid block (or carve-it-yourself) method is considered by many to be the highest form of model-building art. Shaping balsa wood is not as hard as it may seem at first glance; it is easy to work and sand, requiring few tools and little knowledge of sculpting. Sometimes, when a balsa block is not available in the size suitable for a certain model, two blocks are glued together, the joint forming the vertical center line between the two halves of the hull. Keep in mind that cutting in the direction of the wood grain is easier and safer.

Plans show the top view, side view, and end view. The top view is traced onto the block first, followed by cutting, trimming, and sanding. Then the side view (profile) is traced on both sides of that shape, and so forth. With a gouge, the completely shaped hull is hollowed out bit by bit, according to plans. You'll need a bench vise to hold the work securely while shaping. Decking is usually cut out from thin mahogany veneer or plywood, taking precautions against splitting.

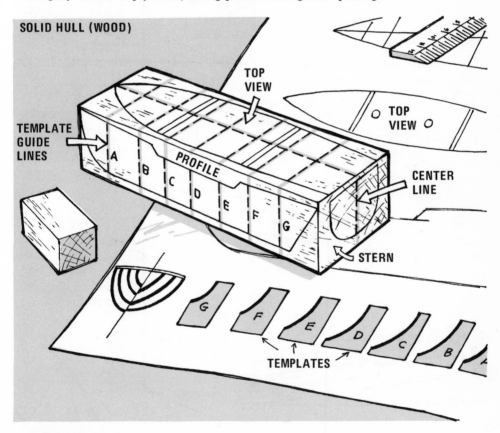

SOLID HULL (WOOD)

Templates are half-section pattern guides that indicate hull contour at various points. You cut them out from the sheet and use them to help in properly shaping the hull's outside. You check your cutting and trimming often, by holding each template against its corresponding station on the hull until it makes a perfect fit.

Familiarizing yourself with the parts goes hand in hand with interpreting the plans for the model. Allow plenty of time to study the drawings until you completely understand the procedure of construction. As you're studying the plans, build the model *in your mind*, step by step. Though you won't foresee everything, such preparation will make your job easier in the long run.

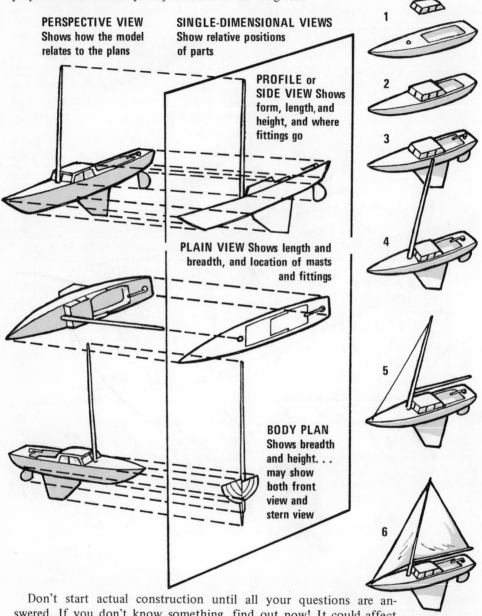

PERSPECTIVE VIEW
Shows how the model relates to the plans

SINGLE-DIMENSIONAL VIEWS
Show relative positions of parts

PROFILE or SIDE VIEW Shows form, length, and height, and where fittings go

PLAIN VIEW Shows length and breadth, and location of masts and fittings

BODY PLAN Shows breadth and height... may show both front view and stern view

Don't start actual construction until all your questions are answered. If you don't know something, find out now! It could affect your procedure in a way you don't foresee at present.

When a plan needs to be enlarged, it can of course be photostated to the desired size. But with a sharp-pointed soft pencil and a ruler, you can make the enlargement yourself. Draw a frame around the plan. Make sure the sides are accurately squared up, that is, every corner a true right angle. Draw a line dividing the frame in half, across; then divide those two spaces in half; keep dividing the new spaces accurately in half until you have enough. Then divide the same way up and down.

Let's say you want a plan twice as large. On separate paper, draw a frame exactly twice the size of the other. That means doubling both length and width so that the resulting frame *appears* to be four times the size of the original. Draw exactly as many divisions as you did before, again dividing in half over and over. The grid lines naturally will be twice as far apart as the lines on the original plan. Wherever the printed boat pattern crosses the grid lines, mark a point on the corresponding spot in the new grid. For sharper curves you'll need more points to obtain the correct shape. Then draw lines from point to point, and you've got a full-size working drawing.

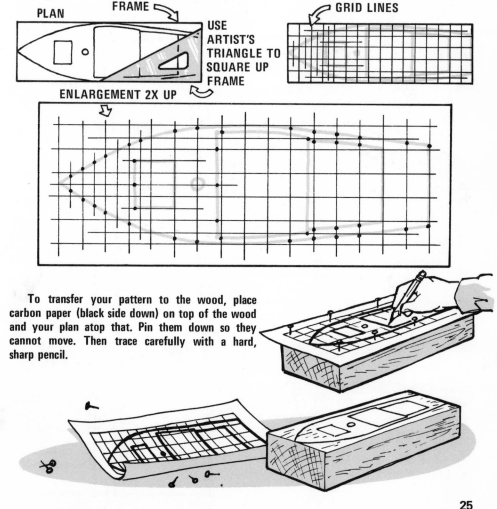

To transfer your pattern to the wood, place carbon paper (black side down) on top of the wood and your plan atop that. Pin them down so they cannot move. Then trace carefully with a hard, sharp pencil.

Masts and booms are made just long enough to support the sails designed for them. *Sail patterns* are your guides for making sails of the correct size and shape. They are somewhat longer than the finished sail will be, to allow for hemming. The pattern includes lines to show where the raw edges of cloth are folded under and sewed with needle and fine thread to form the hems. (Remember that sails for operating models should be slightly slack.) The sails are then laced to masts and booms with heavier line.

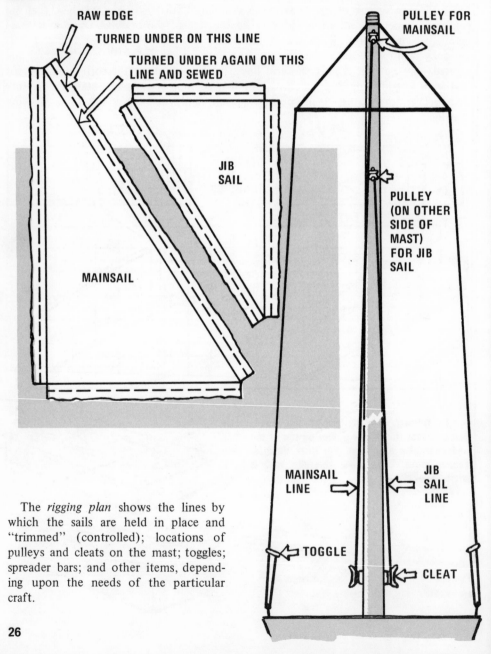

The *rigging plan* shows the lines by which the sails are held in place and "trimmed" (controlled); locations of pulleys and cleats on the mast; toggles; spreader bars; and other items, depending upon the needs of the particular craft.

26

The plans for *preformed plastic kits* have exploded views of the model. They show each separate detail, where it is attached and in what order. Parts are numbered to correspond with the instructions, so you can quickly and easily check the part you are handling with the plan. Exact order of assembly must be followed, otherwise a glued-in piece might get in the way of another step.

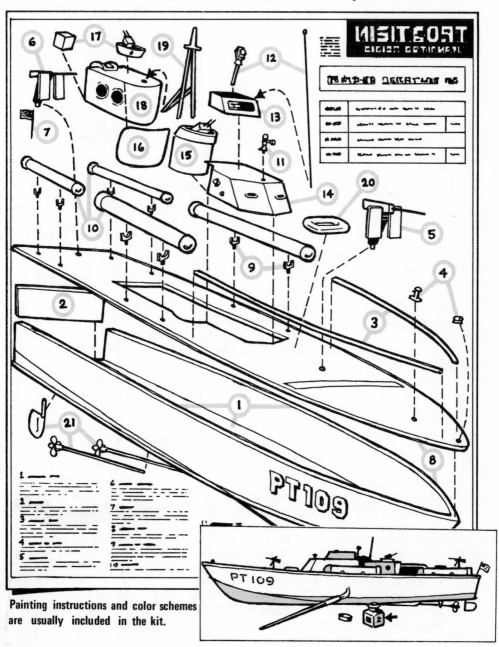

Painting instructions and color schemes are usually included in the kit.

CHAPTER FOUR

Select Your Tools and Materials

After you have planned the operation from beginning to end in your mind, and you are ready for actual construction, you will need an out-of-the-way work area to avoid being disturbed or having the model moved when you're not working on it. A flat working surface is essential. If it's a table top that must be protected from sharp tools and paint, a smooth pine plank atop the table is ideal to work on. To protect your clothes against such things as wood dust, cement, wood sealer, and paint, use a shop apron of thick enough cloth to keep liquids from seeping through.

Assemble everything you'll need for the job. Segregating tools, materials, and parts in separate boxes is the best way to avoid confused and sloppy workmanship. (A portable toolbox is also handy for carrying extra batteries, fuel, cement for repairs, fishline for retrieving models, and other supplies ready for use at the sailing site.) Stow tools carefully, not in a careless jumble. A good workman maintains all his materials in an orderly and organized manner *throughout* the construction process. At quitting time, he cleans the work area, puts away the tools, and leaves the model in a safe condition . . . all signs of good workmanship.

Additional materials, most of which you will find essential to your work, are in the checklist below. Have them on hand.

- ☐ Common pins for holding material in place. For tiny parts use ½" size ("mils") to avoid splitting the wood.
- ☐ Tacks, nails, screws
- ☐ Rubber bands to hold glued parts together
- ☐ Waxed paper to lay over plans in use
- ☐ Single-edged razor blades

- ☐ Cement: waterproof and fuel-proof for gas engines
- ☐ Paint: waterproof
- ☐ Wood sealer
- ☐ Masking tape for neat borders when painting
- ☐ Draftsman's triangle for drawing straight lines
- ☐ Airplane model dope
- ☐ Plastic wood to fill seams

- ☐ Sandpaper assortment: all grades from coarse (for rough shaping) to #00 (for fine finishing)
- ☐ Block for sandpaper
- ☐ Solder and flux for electrical connections
- ☐ Needle and thread for sails and rigging
- ☐ Penknife: optional

There is a tendency in many working situations to use the first implement within hasty reach—a bad practice that can lead to a damaged tool, ruined work, or physical injury. Use a tool only for the kind of work it was intended.

Use The Right Tool For The Right Job

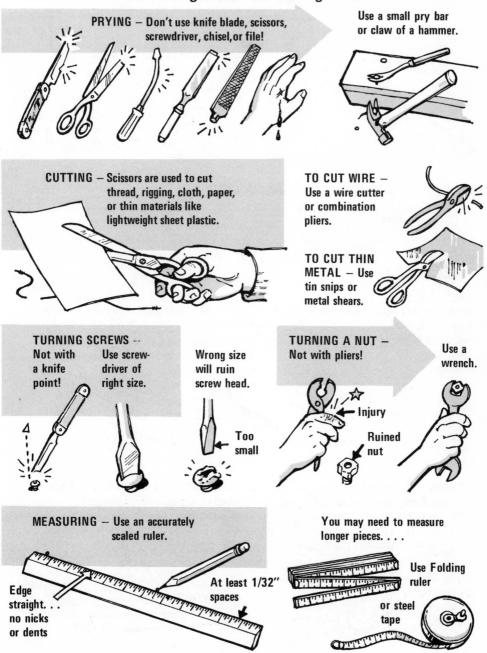

PRYING — Don't use knife blade, scissors, screwdriver, chisel, or file!

Use a small pry bar or claw of a hammer.

CUTTING — Scissors are used to cut thread, rigging, cloth, paper, or thin materials like lightweight sheet plastic.

TO CUT WIRE — Use a wire cutter or combination pliers.

TO CUT THIN METAL — Use tin snips or metal shears.

TURNING SCREWS -- Not with a knife point! Use screwdriver of right size.

Wrong size will ruin screw head.

Too small

TURNING A NUT — Not with pliers!

Use a wrench.

Injury

Ruined nut

MEASURING — Use an accurately scaled ruler.

Edge straight... no nicks or dents

At least 1/32" spaces

You may need to measure longer pieces. . . .

Use Folding ruler

or steel tape

Keep your tools in good working condition: clean, sharp, and reliable. Examine cutting edges often for dullness. Not only will a dull tool spoil your material, but it is difficult and dangerous to work with. Some materials are so tough they take the edge off a tool very quickly. Sharpen all dull edges before settling down to work so you won't have to take time out in the middle of an operation. A *saw*, however, requires expert sharpening; don't tackle it yourself; instead, take it to a hardware store, saw sharpener, or fixit-shop.

DULL Edge shows thin bright line along edge

SHARP Edge — thin bright line is gone

To prevent rust and preserve edges, wipe with oily rag or thin auto cup grease before storing metal tools.

How to Sharpen

Use a *coarse* oilstone to cut an edge down rapidly; then finish with a *fine* oilstone. A *combination stone* is coarse on one side and fine on the other. A tool is sharpened by rubbing the edge *against* the stone—but never rub an edge on a dry stone. Before using, apply a few drops of oil to the stone. Keep the stone level while sharpening.

CHISELS AND PLANE-IRONS — Bear down with hands, and rub back and forth parallel with a full length of stone. Don't dip or scoop!

Keep edge at angle across stone

Bevel level with top of stone

Wipe clean. If line of dullness is gone, turn tool over. . . keep it flat on stone. . .

Give it one or two light sidewise strokes, to remove any burr or wire edge.

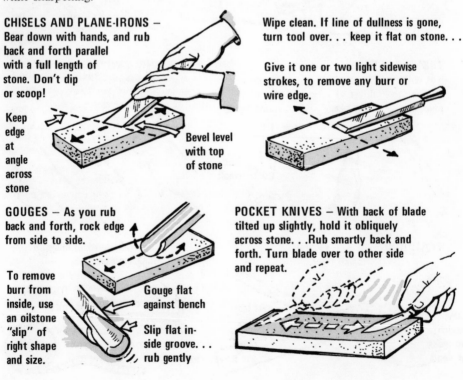

GOUGES — As you rub back and forth, rock edge from side to side.

To remove burr from inside, use an oilstone "slip" of right shape and size.

Gouge flat against bench

Slip flat inside groove. . . rub gently

POCKET KNIVES — With back of blade tilted up slightly, hold it obliquely across stone. . .Rub smartly back and forth. Turn blade over to other side and repeat.

CHAPTER FIVE

Construction Techniques

Never begin actual construction until every single step is clearly understood. If necessary, go over the plans and instructions several times in order to eliminate any error or oversight in the middle of some later operation. Guesswork only leads to unforeseen trouble and vexation.

The examples that follow show some of the steps involved in the various methods of assembly procedure.

WOOD—Precarved Hull—Power Model

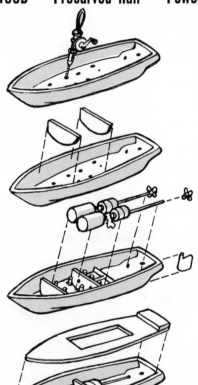

Drill holes for engine mounting bolts, and for propeller-shaft tube and rudder bearing in stern. Sand hull smooth inside and outside, and apply fuel-proof sealer. Paint inside with dope (fuel-proof for internal combustion engines).

Sand and shape bulkheads; brush on dope. Glue them into hull with fuel-proof cement.

Insert shaft tube into stern hole, and glue from outside. Solder electrical connections of power plant; check to see that it works. Affix power plant in hull. Attach shaft and propeller and rudder.

Sand and shape, seal and dope the deck. Cement into place (there should be a hole over the power plant).

Assemble and glue cabin and superstructure parts together. When the cement is dry, corners can be rounded with sandpaper. Then fit the unit over hole in deck. Note that the cabin is removable to provide access to batteries or fuel tank and for starting. With internal combustion engines, the cabin is used only for display; in operation the engine needs plenty of air in order to prevent damage to the power plant.

WOOD—Solid Block Carving

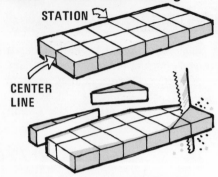

Saw, square up, and plane the block of wood smooth to working size. Draw a *center line* from fore to aft. At right angles to center line, draw in or trace construction guide lines (or *"stations"*) from your plan.

STATION

CENTER LINE

Copy *topside view* of hull from the plan onto the wood. Then neatly saw off excess wood almost to the hull pattern line.

Shave and sand the sides to the pattern line. Mark the station lines again on the new surface.

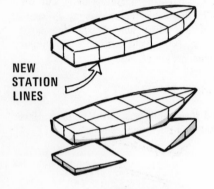

NEW STATION LINES

Copy *hull profile* from plan onto sides of the hull and saw off excess wood at bottom almost to the profile lines.

Nail a temporary block on top of hull to provide a grip for your vise. Turn hull over, then shave off excess wood, shape, and sand outside of hull to pattern lines.

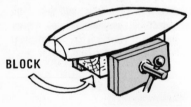

BLOCK

Use *templates* to check hull shape as you trim. Each template must fit at its corresponding station on *both sides* of the hull to achieve correct final shape.

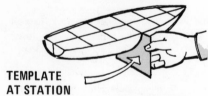

TEMPLATE AT STATION

Templates are hull pattern guides that you trace onto cardboard from your plan and then cut out. Number each template to correspond with its own station line, also numbered on the hull, to prevent error.

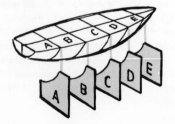

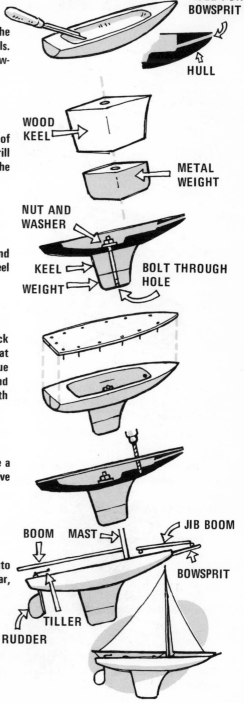

Trace from plan the inside dimensions of the hull. Hollow out to final thickness of hull's walls. Also bore a hole at the prow to receive the bowsprit.

Fashion a keel, consisting of an upper section of wood and a lower section of metal, for weight. Drill a hole through them and into the bottom of the hull.

Fasten keel and weight to hull with bolt, and glue keel and hull together. Also nail hull to keel from inside for added strength.

Shape the *deck* to fit the hull. Then fasten deck to hull with glue and brads. Countersink brads; that is, set them below surface of the deck. After glue dries, fill nail holes with plastic wood or balsa and smooth with sandpaper. Round off deck edges with plane.

Mark location of mast as shown on plan. Bore a hole through deck and part way into hull to receive the mast.

Shape mast, booms, bowsprit, etc., and glue into place according to plan. Form rudder and tiller bar, and attach with fittings.

Attach all hardware. Assemble rigging and sails.

WOOD — "Bread-and-Butter" —also called *laminating* or *lift method*

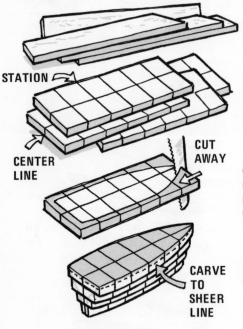

STATION

CENTER LINE

CUT AWAY

CARVE TO SHEER LINE

Lifts are smoothly dressed boards which, when glued together, will form the hull.

On each lift, draw a *center line* from fore to aft and on ends. From the plans, draw or trace construction guide lines (or *"stations"*) ... make sure they are at right angles to center line.

Trace each top view of *hull pattern* onto its corresponding lift from plan. Neatly cut each lift almost to hull pattern and then plane smooth to pattern line. Whenever you cut away construction guide lines, mark them again on new surface.

Trace each *profile outline* of boat from plan onto its corresponding lift. Carve top lift to *sheer line*.

Saw out inside of hull on lifts indicated on plans. You can finish hollowing inside after entire model is glued together.

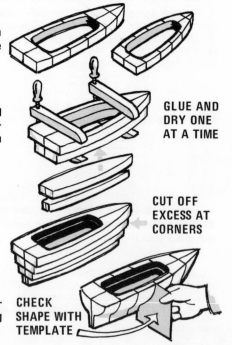

GLUE AND DRY ONE AT A TIME

CUT OFF EXCESS AT CORNERS

CHECK SHAPE WITH TEMPLATE

Glue lifts together: start with two, spreading glue on facing surfaces. Clamp them together securely until dry. Add the remaining lifts, one at a time, in the same way.

Shave square edges from assembled lifts.

Round them off to final shape until all templates fit at their corresponding stations.

Finish hollowing out inside of hull ... and continue construction as with solid block carving method.

WOOD—Machine Carved Hull

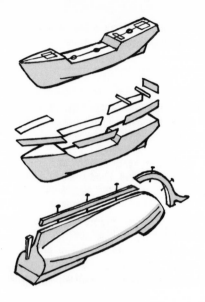

Sand smooth all surfaces of preshaped hull. Mark a center line along deck, and guide lines for superstructure and fittings. Drill holes for mast.

Sand and shape bulwarks and side rails. Glue them evenly to hull in line with hull contour. Hold until cement dries.

Glue keel, sternpost, and stem to bottom, hold in place with pins or nails. Nails can be removed later and holes filled with plastic wood.

WOOD—Plank-on-Frame

Keel is a solid piece slotted halfway down. Number each slot to match bulkhead pieces, to prevent error when gluing.

Bulkheads slide into slots. Check fit before gluing. Glue straight and evenly into place. Wait until dry.

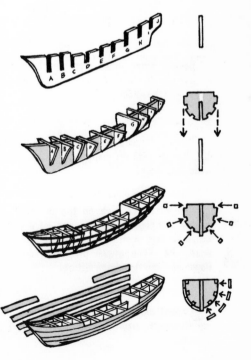

Add stringers. Stringers give shape and surface for planking. Glue into notches from bow to stern. Keep curve smooth and square with deck. Sand ends to fit at bow. Let dry.

Cut and fit planking around hull. Starting at the bottom, glue planking from rear toward front. Make sure each piece fits before gluing. When cement has dried, sand planking and seal the seams.

WOOD—Precut Hull and Superstructure

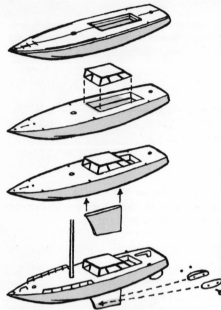

Sand hull smooth. Mark guide lines for superstructure. Drill holes for masts, rudder housing, and other fittings.

Try out cabin parts for good fit. Glue carefully in place and let dry. Sand glued joints smooth.

Sand and shape keel; then fit and glue along bottom center line of hull. Sand and seal boat ready for painting.

Sand mast to taper toward top. Insert glue-covered end into hole, making sure that front view of mast is straight up and down and profile view correctly raked. Hold firmly until dry. Attach rudder. Paint and finish boat. Then attach keel weights.

PLASTIC—Prefabricated Parts

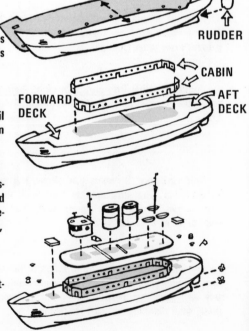

Cement along inside seam and hold two halves of hull together with rubber bands. While cement is tacky, attach rudder.

Cement forward main deck to hull; hold until dry. Repeat with aft main deck. Cement main cabin walls onto deck.

Cement upper deck on top of cabin. Paint assembly completed thus far, and let dry. Paint and fasten fittings, such as smokestacks, pilothouse, lifeboats, etc. Then attach propellers, anchor hoist, flagpoles, and remaining fittings.

Cement masts and spars into place. Finish painting. Use plastic paint.

DO-IT-RIGHT Construction Tips

USING THE PLANS

When model parts have to be laid on top of the plan and held in place for accurate assembly guidance, that plan needs protection against tearing, scratching, and smudging. Here's the way to do it:

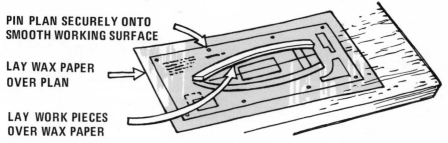

PIN PLAN SECURELY ONTO
SMOOTH WORKING SURFACE

LAY WAX PAPER
OVER PLAN

LAY WORK PIECES
OVER WAX PAPER

When *measuring* and *working* as directed by the plan, be accurate! Otherwise you will find that parts don't fit the way they should and you end up with a slipshod job—or your project may even be brought to a dead stop.

When the job calls for *square* corners or crossed lines, don't guess at it. It must be absolutely square: a 90° angle. Use *good* measuring and marking equipment. And use care not to drop, twist, or nick these precision tools, nor to run cutting blades against plastic edges.

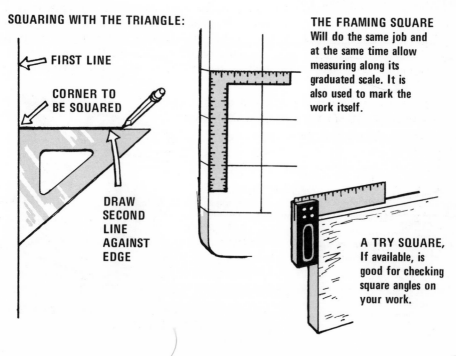

SQUARING WITH THE TRIANGLE:

FIRST LINE

CORNER TO
BE SQUARED

DRAW
SECOND
LINE
AGAINST
EDGE

THE FRAMING SQUARE
Will do the same job and at the same time allow measuring along its graduated scale. It is also used to mark the work itself.

A TRY SQUARE,
If available, is good for checking square angles on your work.

To draw long curves *true* is next to impossible to do freehand. Equipment is available for that purpose, if you can afford it. The *adjustable curve ruler* is easily bent to any desired curve. It stays curved without being held, so you can draw a smooth curve along its metal edge. The plastic *spline* used by professionals requires *spline weights* to hold the curve in place. A set of weights is expensive, while the adjustable curve ruler is fairly inexpensive. However, you can make your own spline from a strip of flexible wood, planed smooth and tapered at both ends.

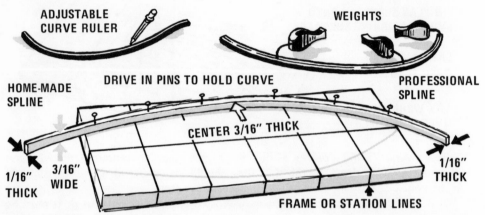

ADJUSTABLE CURVE RULER

WEIGHTS

HOME-MADE SPLINE

DRIVE IN PINS TO HOLD CURVE

PROFESSIONAL SPLINE

CENTER 3/16" THICK

1/16" THICK 3/16" WIDE

1/16" THICK

FRAME OR STATION LINES

The shaping of the underpart of the hull is the most important part of constructing an operational boat. Plans for building your own hull include scaled drawings of hull dimensions and contour at various measured points (stations) along its length. By transferring these drawings to cardboard or sheet metal and carefully cutting each shape in half, you will have accurate templates to guide you in the shaping of your hull. You can also make a template of the full hull length and of the bow shape. Make frequent checks with templates during shaping. Fit the same template at its station on both sides of the hull so that the hull's shape will be exactly the same on both sides.

USING ONLY HALF OF CROSS-SECTION DRAWINGS, CUT OUT SEPARATE TEMPLATE FOR EACH STATION LINE.

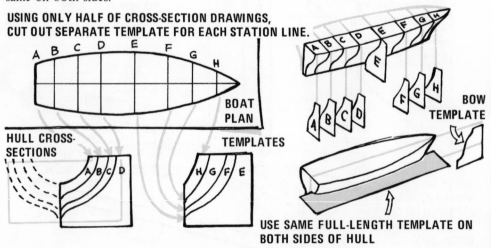

A B C D E F G H

BOAT PLAN

BOW TEMPLATE

HULL CROSS-SECTIONS

TEMPLATES

USE SAME FULL-LENGTH TEMPLATE ON BOTH SIDES OF HULL

THE WOOD

During construction, pay attention to the direction of the wood grain so you can use it to best advantage. Wood is stronger in the grain direction, weaker across the grain. A long, thin piece of wood should be cut so its length runs with the grain. With soft balsa, however, against-the-grain weakness has the advantage of greater flexibility. especially when soaked with hot water.

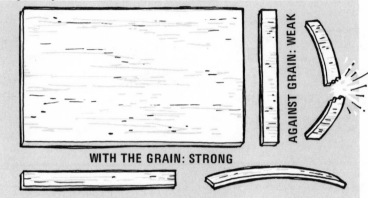

Dowel sticks come in 3-foot lengths and 1/8 inch to 1 1/4 inch diameter sizes. Only those pieces with a straight grain will permit smooth planing on all sides. Sometimes one end of the stick will be straight-grained and the other end cross-grained.

Steam bending will give dowels, stringers, and planks a gentle curve. Keep the stick in boiling water for 15 to 20 minutes. While still hot and steaming, bend and hold it in the desired shape on a form until completely dry and cool.

DRIVE NAILS INTO
BOARD TO HOLD
STEAMED PIECES
IN CURVED SHAPE
UNTIL DRY

There is another method of bending sheet plywood into shape. Heat an electric iron, but not hot enough to burn the wood. With a clean paint brush, thoroughly wet the outside curve of the wood. Iron along the inside curve—the idea being that dry heat contracts one side while water expands the other. Keep wetting and ironing until the curve is attained. Then keep ironing until the wet side is thoroughly dry; this will retain the curve long enough to let you fasten the piece into place on the model.

WATER

A curved piece can also be made from two or three straight pieces of wood. Copy or trace the curve pattern onto the wood pieces, making sure that you will be cutting in the direction of the grain. Cut the pieces to shape and plane smooth. Before gluing them together, see that they will fit their station on the model. Glue the pieces together, and clamp until dry and ready to be attached to the model.

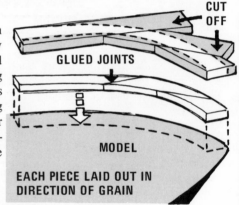

CUT OFF

GLUED JOINTS

MODEL

EACH PIECE LAID OUT IN DIRECTION OF GRAIN

HOLDING THE WORK

When sawing, shaping, gouging, planing, filing, drilling, or soldering model parts, the work should be held rigidly in a vise. Small metal parts especially are practically impossible to hold firmly enough by hand for filing or sawing. Care must always be taken that the work is not marred by the vise itself.

WHEN SHAPING A SOLID HULL, A WOOD BLOCK TEMPORARILY NAILED TO DECK KEEPS WORK CLEAR OF VISE JAWS

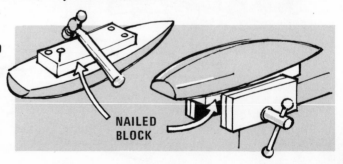

NAILED BLOCK

A *cradle* is used to hold the hull in a vise while gouging inside the hull. Although the vise will hold the hull without a cradle, the device makes gouging much easier. The cradle can be used during other steps of construction, too. To make a cradle, you can use the waste pieces left over when you sawed the hull out of the original block; fasten them to a base of rough board.

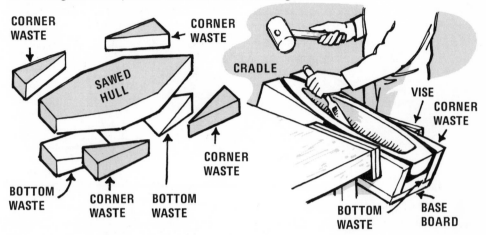

"C" clamps (or *cabinet clamps*) can be used to hold two or more glued items together rigidly until the cement dries. Be careful not to screw the clamp so tightly that the work is crushed. When soldering metal, clamping the parts to be joined leaves both your hands free for the operation.

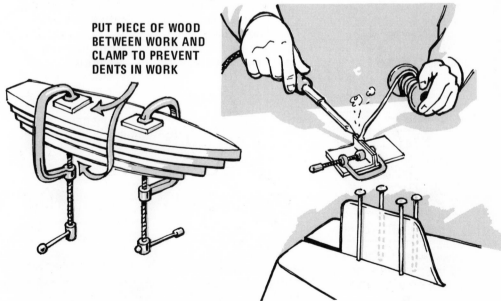

Pins (common dressmaker type) are used to hold parts in position during construction, and to hold glued pieces together while drying.

CUTTING, CARVING, AND SHAPING

The *ripsaw* is used for sawing *with* the grain. Never use a ripsaw to cut against the grain, for it would haggle the grain and break off surface bits of wood near the edge of the cut.

The *crosscut saw* is used for sawing *across* the grain. Avoid using this saw to cut with the grain, for the teeth would be forced back in straight and the saw would lose its set.

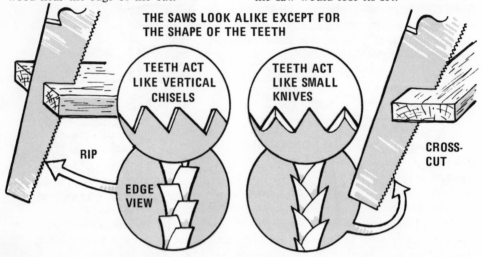

THE SAWS LOOK ALIKE EXCEPT FOR THE SHAPE OF THE TEETH

TEETH ACT LIKE VERTICAL CHISELS

TEETH ACT LIKE SMALL KNIVES

RIP

CROSS-CUT

EDGE VIEW

Start a rip cut near point of blade and lightly draw saw toward you. Then use easy, straight, full-length strokes.

Start a cross cut near heel of blade with a few light upstrokes until groove is formed. Then use long easy, straight strokes.

To keep saw perfectly vertical for a square cut, check angle often with try square held against blade.

THUMB SUPPORTS SIDE OF BLADE

DON'T LET WASTE PIECE DROP

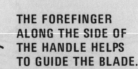

THE FOREFINGER ALONG THE SIDE OF THE HANDLE HELPS TO GUIDE THE BLADE.

To prevent splintering on underside when cut is almost completed, support waste side of work — and don't twist it off with saw.

The *coping saw* is used to cut curves in thin wood. Shift the work around so the saw can accommodate the curves it meets. When making sharp turns, change the blade's angle in the frame to avoid breaking the blade. To avoid overheating the blade make your strokes as long as possible. When placing a blade in the frame, have the teeth pointing toward the handle.

The *compass saw* is used to cut circles, and curves where the coping saw's frame prevents sawing. Cut plywood nearly to the construction line, then plane and sandpaper down to the line.

ALWAYS SAW ON WASTE SIDE OF DRAWN LINE, INSTEAD OF HALVING IT

The *keyhole saw* has a blade like the compass saw, but smaller and narrower. It is used mostly for small work and in close quarters.

FIRST DRILL HOLE FROM WHICH TO START CUTTING

Chisels and gouges are precision tools—keep them razor sharp to do their job and keep their edges protected. Cut only wood with them, never anything else. And never pry with them. Use a wooden *mallet* with these tools; a metal hammer will splinter the handle. Be sure to mark off the area to be hollowed before you start cutting. To do a good job, don't hurry—just cut away little pieces at a time. Your left hand helps to guide the cut and applies pressure. With a gouge, use a twisting motion as well as a digging movement.

DEEP CUTS – Use socket chisel.

First drive straight down to right depth at each end of cutting area.

Then, holding chisel at angle, bevel side down, work chisel back along cutting area. Make cuts 1/8" apart, but not to full depth.

LIGHT TAPS FOR ACCURACY

PARING CUTS —
To clean out deep cuts

First rake out chips with a claw hammer. Then, with chisel, cut only thin slices.

For clean flat cuts, use slightly diagonal strokes, with the grain.

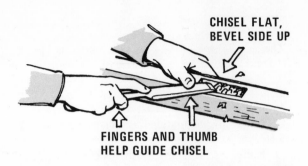

CHISEL FLAT, BEVEL SIDE UP

FINGERS AND THUMB HELP GUIDE CHISEL

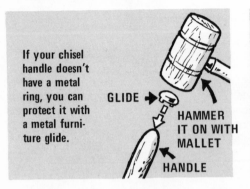

If your chisel handle doesn't have a metal ring, you can protect it with a metal furniture glide.

GLIDE

HAMMER IT ON WITH MALLET

HANDLE

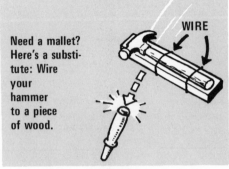

Need a mallet? Here's a substitute: Wire your hammer to a piece of wood.

WIRE

Skillful *planing* comes with practice. With long smooth strokes, try to get shavings to come off in continuous ribbons, the thinner the better. Never drag the plane backwards with the blade touching the wood; after each stroke lift the plane back ready for the next stroke. Sight down the board for high spots and check often with a try square for uneven work. Always keep the *plane iron* sharp, for a dull iron will tear wood rather than shave it. When planing plywood, use extra care not to fray the surface veneer at the edges.

BLOCK PLANE
Used mostly for end grain and for small pieces of wood.

Shave from edge to middle, to avoid splitting off splinters at edges.

SMOOTH PLANE
(Larger than block plane)

Though it may also be used for edges and ends, it is meant for shaving with the grain on broad surfaces, and for finishing work ready for sandpapering.

JACK PLANE
(Larger than smooth plane)

For all-around work.

Stroke edges with the grain. Plane should be held slightly diagonal to direction of cut.

Use a *file* to shape and smooth rudders, propellers, and the many other *metal* parts you will be shaping. You can also use a file to adapt miniature lifeboats, davits, deck winches, and other fittings to your particular model. New files need breaking in, so use them first on large surfaces until the teeth are worn. And keep your files in clean working condition by stroking them after use with a *file card*, a sort of wire brush with short, stiff bristles.

THESE ARE THE SMALL FILE SHAPES YOU WILL FIND MOST USEFUL:

ROUND

HALF-ROUND

TRIANGULAR

FLAT

COARSE FILING
...when you want to remove a lot of metal fast. Stroke forward. . .lift file clear on backstroke; dragging back dulls teeth.

LIGHT FILING
File toward edge first. Then away from edge for light touching up. Lift, don't drag, on return stroke.

MOST FILING IS DONE ON WORK HELD IN A VISE.

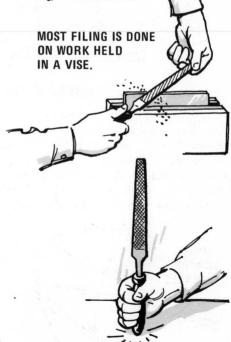

VISE

Sometimes it is more convenient to stroke the object to be filed against the stationary file, instead of the other way around.

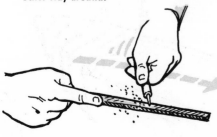

TO ATTACH HANDLE
Insert tang, rap handle on firm surface to force tang deeper into handle.

Use *sandpaper* to shape pieces to exact size and to smooth surfaces after they have been shaped with cutting tools. To sand a wood surface flat, a job that cannot be done perfectly by holding the sandpaper in your fingers, use a *sanding block.* You can easily make one yourself.

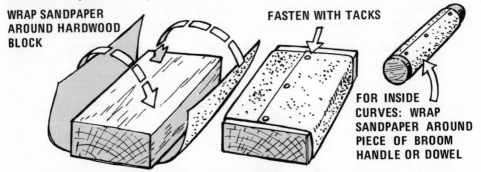

WRAP SANDPAPER AROUND HARDWOOD BLOCK

FASTEN WITH TACKS

FOR INSIDE CURVES: WRAP SANDPAPER AROUND PIECE OF BROOM HANDLE OR DOWEL

To remove waste from *sheet plastic* parts: scribe a line three or four times along the piece to be trimmed, without cutting through. Cut one-inch wide sections from the scribed line to the edge of the sheet. Bend the sections down—they'll snap off cleanly.

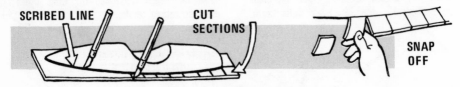

SCRIBED LINE

CUT SECTIONS

SNAP OFF

CEMENTING AND FASTENING

Make sure your cement is smooth and free of flakes or other particles that might prevent adhesion of the parts to be joined. For wood, airplane-model cement is fine; plastic cement is for joining plastic only. Keep the cap on the cement tube not in use; to prevent clogging while in use, keep a nail in the open mouth of the tube. When joining narrow edges or small parts, apply a thin film of cement to *both* the surfaces to be joined, press together firmly, and wipe away excess cement. The joined parts may be held tightly with rubber bands or tied together with string until dry.

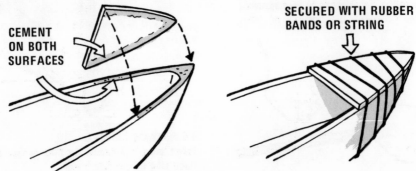

CEMENT ON BOTH SURFACES

SECURED WITH RUBBER BANDS OR STRING

When gluing larger areas together, spread a thin, even sheet over the *entire* joining areas of *both* surfaces. Then clamp together firmly enough to eliminate any air bubbles and to ensure good surface-to-surface contact. The more pressure you apply—but not to the point of crushing the work—the stronger the joint will be. Use enough clamps to do the job. Wipe away excess cement before it hardens. With bread-and-butter constructions, glue and clamp only one lift at a time, and let dry before adding the next line.

Here is one way to insure perfect fit and to prevent splitting of the wood. Before gluing the pieces in place, fit them together exactly and clamp temporarily. Drill several pilot holes completely through the first piece and barely into the other. Then drive some brads through the holes and slightly into the second piece. When you separate the pieces, leave the brads sticking through the first piece and spread glue on both surfaces to be joined. Rejoin the pieces; the brads will quickly find their holes and match the pieces accurately together. When the cemented union holds securely, you can remove the brads.

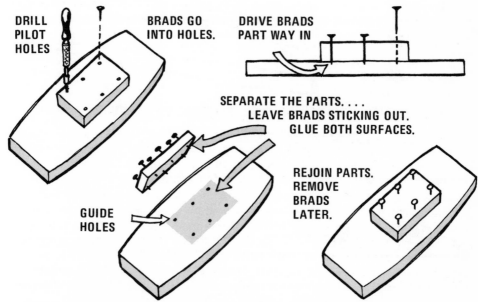

DRILL PILOT HOLES

BRADS GO INTO HOLES.

DRIVE BRADS PART WAY IN

SEPARATE THE PARTS. . . .
LEAVE BRADS STICKING OUT.
GLUE BOTH SURFACES.

GUIDE HOLES

REJOIN PARTS. REMOVE BRADS LATER.

It is always a good idea to drill *pilot holes* into the work before driving in nails or screws . . . it prevents splitting. Be sure to make the pilot holes a little narrower than the diameter of the fastening. Wood is also apt to split if you drive in a lot of fastenings close together or all in the same line with the grain. So stagger them slightly, and don't use too many.

You can prepare a screw to drive home much more easily if you lubricate it with soap . . . pushing it into a bar of soap will do the trick.

SCREW IN SOAP

MASTS, BOOMS, AND SPARS

Use only clean and straight-grained sticks or dowels, free from knots or splits. Sticks should also be squared true and a little longer and thicker than needed. Store sticks and dowels flat and straight until ready for use so they won't be bent permanently out of shape.

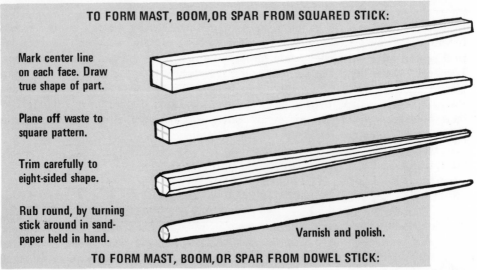

TO FORM MAST, BOOM, OR SPAR FROM SQUARED STICK:

Mark center line on each face. Draw true shape of part.

Plane off waste to square pattern.

Trim carefully to eight-sided shape.

Rub round, by turning stick around in sand-paper held in hand.

Varnish and polish.

TO FORM MAST, BOOM, OR SPAR FROM DOWEL STICK:

First mark the center at each end of the stick. Then sand (or if dowel is too thick, plane carefully) to tapered shape. If you shave it down before cutting off the waste ends, you'll have more stick to hold onto while working. Finish off and smooth with coarse sandpaper, and then with fine sandpaper, held in your palm.

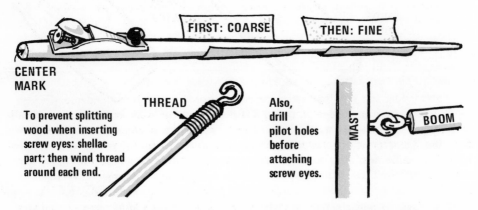

FIRST: COARSE   THEN: FINE

CENTER MARK

To prevent splitting wood when inserting screw eyes: shellac part; then wind thread around each end.

THREAD

Also, drill pilot holes before attaching screw eyes.

MAST   BOOM

When attaching masts to hull, make sure they are in line with the hull, fore and aft. If you find that a mast hole is not true in the center line, ream it out a bit larger on one side and jam a little wooden wedge in the hole to push and hold the mast at dead center.

SAILS

Lay out your sail pattern on heavy paper. Transfer the pattern to the cloth, allowing for extra material along the edges for double-folding the hems. Then fold the edges over and stitch with needle and fine thread.

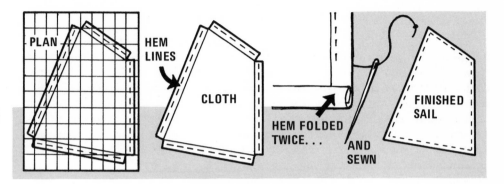

PLAN | HEM LINES | CLOTH | HEM FOLDED TWICE... AND SEWN | FINISHED SAIL

SEALING AND PAINTING

First of all, check the entire hull for crevices, nicks, and other flaws. On wood other than balsa, fill all the imperfections with *plastic wood.* Sand smooth when dry and hard. On balsa, use *plastic balsa* (not plastic wood—it dries to a different hardness that prevents good sanding).

SEALING WORKING MODELS—WOOD. Since the boat will be operating in water, its hull must be absolutely watertight and impervious to seepage on all surfaces, both inside and outside. The smallest scratch or bare spot will admit water into the wood pores to swell and distort the wood, loosen joints, and cause paint and undercoat to blister, scale, or crack. Therefore, before any paint is applied to new wood the grain must be thoroughly sealed. Trying to seal wood with several layers of paint is useless; paint alone will not seal the wood grain tight enough for boating operations. Although about four coats should suffice, the more coats of sealer applied, the finer and tougher your model's finish will be. You can't apply too much. Between coats, after each one dries, sand it lightly.

Wet sanding the last few sealer coats will produce the finest undercoating for a top-notch paint job. This is done with an abrasive-coated sheet of plastic which is very smooth and waterproof. The water lubricates the abrasive, thus preventing scratching of the surface and giving a much smoother surface than dry sanding does. Wet sanding is used after the last dry sanding operation, when you are sure water seepage is no longer a factor. Apply another sealer coat and start your wet sanding: Dip the abrasive-coated sheet in water until very wet, then sand. At intervals, wipe away the resultant pasty mixture with a soft cloth. Keep the abrasive-coated sheet wet and clean by dipping regularly in water.

SEALING BALSA WOOD. Due to its pulpy consistency, balsa is easier to cut and sand—and harder to seal. So use a *balsa grain sealer* or *balsa filler coat* . . . quick drying. It is easy to apply and to sandpaper.

SEALING POWERED BOATS. Special attention has to be given to sealing hull interior surfaces carefully because a certain amount of water is likely to seep past shafts and tubes into the hull. Inner surfaces of *internal combustion engine* and *glow-plug engine* models must be sealed with *fuel-proof* sealer only. With internal combustion engines, other sealers would permit fuel and exhaust to seep into bare wood, both deteriorating the hull and creating a fire hazard. With glow-plug engines, the alcohol fuel would dissolve any other kind of sealer.

PAINTING WORKING MODELS—WOOD. Paint and varnish, besides being decorative, help to preserve wooden hulls, decks, and superstructures, and to keep water from swelling and loosening joints. Don't start to paint until you are wholly confident about your sealing finish. To separate colors neatly and sharply, press a strip of *masking tape* (a pressure-sensitive adhesive paper, usually tan, available in several widths) along the line of separation. To protect the deck, tape along the edge on top. Run a fingernail carefully along the tape edges to make sure they stick firmly, so no paint will seep under to spoil the color line. (Store your tape in a closed container. A dusty tape edge can also spoil the color line.)

Sand all but the last coat of paint with fine wet sandpaper. After each coat dries, rub in the direction of the wood grain, lightly enough not to cut through. As you have noticed, the finest finish takes a lot of elbow grease. The last few coats should be thinned a little with *paint thinner*, or *dope thinner* when painting with dope. Remove the masking tape only after paint has thoroughly dried. Apply a new strip of tape for the next color on the other side of the line. For good brush care, clean in thinner and then in warm water and soap after each time used, and hang up to dry.

Colored model-airplane dope is very much in popular use for painting. It dries fast to a tough, lacquerlike finish, alcohol- and waterproof. It is best to use dope of the same make as the sealer to prevent any possible bad chemical reaction between the two. Quick-drying dope should be *flowed* onto the surface with a *filled* brush, not brushed smooth as with slow-drying enamels and paints. On mahogany tops, use *clear* dope. Surfaces can be brought to an even finer gloss by using *rubber compound* over well-dried paint. It is gently rubbed into a small area at a time with a wad of absorbent cotton, and finally polished with soft flannel.

PAINTING DISPLAY MODELS—WOOD. Waterproofing, of course, is not needed, but the pores of new wood need a filler before varnishing, or a primer coat when painting. Try not to paint any surface that still has to be glued. Paint or varnish in thin coats, well brushed out. Between thoroughly dried coats, sand lightly as previously described. For the finest finish, after the last coat, rub down with commercial rubbing compound, powdered rottenstone, or pumice stone.

PAINTING PLASTIC MODELS. Do not use dope; use paint or enamel suitable for plastic surfaces. And don't rush the assembly—pay attention to the many parts that must be painted before being cemented into place.

POWER PLANTS

RUBBER-BAND MOTOR: It is the simplest power source for smaller boats (not over 22 inches). Its quickly spent energy limits the boat to a short run. The motor may be wound up by the propeller or with a simple crank. It can be installed inside the hull, or attached under the hull; or the fuselage of a stick-model airplane can be mounted on top of the boat.

SPRING MOTOR. It is easily installed in smaller boats. The propeller shaft must be lined up accurately with the motor shaft. You can use spring motors taken out of inexpensive toy vehicles, or you can buy complete spring motor assemblies.

GAS ENGINE. An air-cooled engine must receive sufficient breeze to function efficiently. If the hull is not open and shallow, then holes must be cut through the deck or in the cowl or cockpit for ventilation and to prevent warping of wood or plastic. The engine must be mounted so that it is held rigidly in the boat. First, measure the engine for mounting before you cut slots in the bulkhead for it. Cement and screw the mounts to the bulkhead. Then screw the motor to the mounts. Remember to drill pilot holes for the screws, to prevent splitting the wood.

GLOW-PLUG ENGINE. This engine's popularity is due to its light weight and ease of operation. You will need a *flywheel* starter; your dealer may recommend the right one for your particular engine. The fuel used is alcohol with an additive. Spilled fuel and sticky exhaust splatter may require that the cockpit or engine chamber be lined with balsa sheet or mahogany veneer for handier cleaning.

ELECTRIC MOTOR. Power is supplied by *dry cells* (flashlight batteries), or the larger *lantern battery* which lasts somewhat longer, or by a *wet cell* battery (similar to an automobile battery) which can be recharged overnight. To hold batteries firmly in place, you will have to construct a *battery box* from sheet balsa or plywood; or you can buy a *battery holder* which may eliminate some operating problems.

Solder all wiring connections to the electric motor, and to the switch and battery box. *Soft* solder, with its lower melting point, is best for ship model work. With solder you must use *flux*, which cleans away oxide from metal and prevents more from forming. The two main types are *acid flux* which you must *not* use for electrical work and *rosin flux* which you *must* use. Core solder has a center filled with the flux. To guarantee the best results, have a tin of rosin handy. Then, even when using flux-filled solder, apply some extra rosin to the work before soldering.

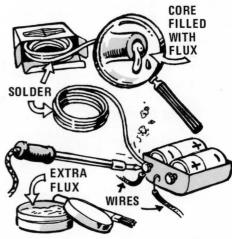

CORE FILLED WITH FLUX

SOLDER

EXTRA FLUX

WIRES

CHAPTER SIX

Operation and Care

SAILBOATS

Skill in the art of sailing comes with practice and patience, and by experimentation with sail and spar adjustments. The following navigational tips apply to a full-size boat operated by a man aboard but, the fundamentals being the same, they will help you with your miniature boat maneuvers. The *boom* line in each figure shows how the mainsail should be "trimmed," that is, how a sail should be slackened or hauled in (tightened) to make the best use of the angle at which wind strikes the boat. Experiment with your model to find the best trim for different courses.

FAVORABLE WINDS — Boat said to be "running free"....

SAIL
BOOM
WIND DEAD ASTERN

AWEATHER OR SCUDDING: Sailing with the wind. You'll sail fairly well with the wind aft but you won't always get the best speed. Steering is difficult when running before the wind, especially in rough water, and there is the danger of the sail jibing over into the water. When scudding, the mainsail (and mizzen, third sail from bow) should be slackened out as far as it will go.

WIND ON THE QUARTER

THREE-QUARTER SAILING. This course is very effective in *rough* water. Rather than sailing aweather, haul in the "sheet" (sail) so you have the wind on one quarter. Following this course awhile, "take the other tack," that is, carefully jibe over to bring the wind on to the other quarter.

REACHING: Sailing with the wind forward of the beam, but not so much as to compel tacking. On a *broad reach*, your boat will continue to run at a good speed. Jib sails should be pulled fairly tight, while the mainsail (and mizzen) should be slack, but not so slack as when sailing with the wind.

WIND ABAFT THE BEAM

WIND ABEAM

WIND FORWARD OF THE BEAM

"REACHING BROAD"

BEATING TO WINDWARD — Sailing against the wind...

WIND AHEAD

SAILING CLOSE HAULED: Bringing your boat as close *into* the wind as possible, while still keeping the sail filled with wind so as to maintain your course at good speed. Smooth water usually permits you to sail closer to the wind than does rough water. If you're hauled too close, however, the sail will begin to flap and you'll lose headway. At the first sign of trembling in the sail, reverse helm (rudder) until wind fills sail.

TACKING: Zigzag runs or laps, the only way to sail against the wind. At the end of the first lap, turn your bow on a small angle so the wind is on opposite side of boat, and start your second lap. Tacking makes progress slow and adds a greater distance to your destination; but it will provide fun and experience.

POWERED MODELS

A *free-running* boat needs a large expanse of relatively calm water. Two-inch ripples are rough water for your miniature, the same as two-foot or higher waves are for full-size speedboats. You are the skipper of a high-speed craft; like any captain worth his salt, use common sense and caution, and take no chances. Let your boat run free only where no bathers or boaters are present, for the safety of both your craft and other people. Before a run, be sure to check the water's depth . . . you wouldn't want to hit bottom and have your propeller, shaft, and strut bent beyond repair! Make your first test on a straight course at moderate speed; you could follow it in a power boat; a rowboat may be too slow.

If a boating pond is not large enough for straight runs, you can install a *fuel shut-off timer* in your fuel supply line, which limits running time to prevent running aground. Or you can set your rudder for circling and launch *parallel* to the shore or dock so the boat will circle out and return without danger of beaching or bumping. A *tether* allows the best controlled method of circling. The model is attached to a pole by the tether (strong string, fishing line, or fine wire, anywhere from ten to twenty-five feet in length). The pole is rigidly fixed into the bottom of the pond. The running line is attached to a *swivel* at the top of the pole (you might use a nail and a ring, but a ball-bearing cap is much better). A *bridle* connects the boat hull to the running line.

STARTING: Remember, an internal combustion engine *needs air!* If your model has a cabin or cover for display purposes, *remove it before starting.* Always hold your boat out of the water when starting the engine. Flip the flywheel smartly with your finger to turn the crankshaft. Many flywheels have a groove into which a string is wound and then pulled for starting. Be patient—it may take several spins to get it going.

LAUNCHING: Once started, disconnect the starting battery, and set the fuel-timer (if you are using one). It is best not to hold a running engine stationary longer than thirty seconds, for it would overheat the power plant. Place the boat *very slowly* in the water; too sudden a load on the engine when the propeller hits the water will make it stall. When you've got the hull floating, launch it with a forward motion to prevent stalling. Electric motor models are started by simply turning the motor switch and launching. All models can be stopped in their paths simply by catching them with your hand.

RACING: Free-style racing is usual with small engines. Large engines are usually restricted to tethered racing in the shallow (3-foot depth) part of a lake or in a pool constructed for that purpose. The racer's speed is calculated by recording the time it takes to complete a specified number of laps, or circles around the post.

PAMPER YOUR BOAT! Give it the same care and attention to detail that you put into its construction. You surely want it to have trouble-free performance and a long life. A model power boat is lightly built for speed—don't let it soak for hours in the water. After its run, wipe it dry inside and out to keep the hull true and in good shape.

Keep working parts and propeller bearings well lubricated with light machine oil.

Pack stern tubes with petroleum jelly (Vaseline), to lubricate and to seal the shaft against entry of water.

In glow-plug engines, wipe away sticky exhaust splatter and spilled fuel from cockpit interiors and hull after each run.

With electric motors, make periodic checks of motor and gears, and lubricate with light machine oil to reduce wear and prolong life.

Take along a small tool chest on boating operations. You may need extra batteries or fuel, a fishline to retrieve a stalled boat, cement for repairs, wrenches to tighten a cylinder head, to change a plug, or to fasten a flywheel or propeller.

If yours is a display model, do not leave it in the hot sun—seams may weaken and come apart. With proper care, no repair or restoration will be necessary.

It is customary to display a model showing the starboard (right) side.

HAPPY SAILING!

CHAPTER SEVEN

Handy Facts

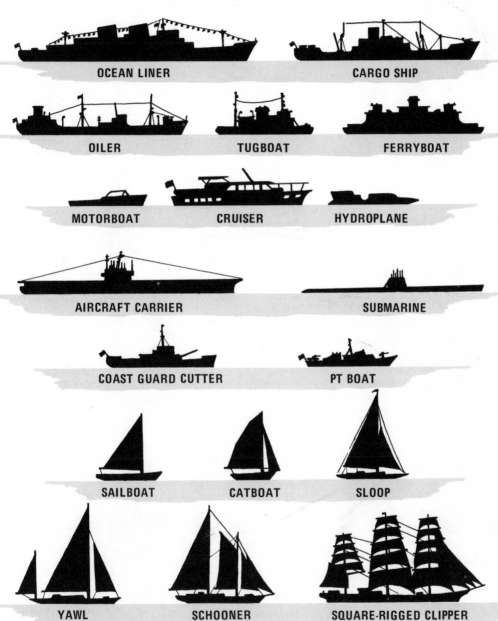

Boats and ships are typified by shape, size, or some other feature. Get to know these silhouettes and you'll be able to identify the craft by name.

TOOLS

ILLUSTRATION	NAME	FUNCTION		CAUTION
	BRUSHES	Painting, Trimming		Always Clean Brushes After Using.
	C-CLAMPS	Holding Two or More Pieces of Wood While Gluing or Bending.		To Prevent Dents, Use a Piece of Wood Between Work and Clamp.
	CHISELS AND GOUGES	Cutting into, Gouging, Shaping.		Hold Chisel Very Tightly in Hand. Use Wooden Mallet.
	HAND SCREWS	Clamping Large Pieces Being Glued Together.		Don't Turn So Tightly That It Crushes the Wood.
	SPRING CLOTHES PINS	Clamps, Small Pieces Together (Shape Jaws if Necessary).		Do Not Get Fingers Caught Between Ends.
	COPING SAW	Cutting Intricate Shapes		Do Not Twist or Bend Blade. Protect Hands.
	DIVIDER	Transferring Dimensions		Be Careful of Very Sharp Points.
	FILES	Taking Off Rough Edges, Smoothing Surfaces, Shaping Metal.		Use Handle! File at Angle When Wood Is Thin.
	HAND DRILL	Drilling Small Holes		Hold Drill Straight and Tightly. Do Not Bend or Twist.

TOOLS

ILLUSTRATION	NAME	FUNCTION		CAUTION
	JEWELER'S OR TACK HAMMER	Driving Dowel Pins, Nails, Etc.		Be Sure Head Is on Tightly. Keep Fingers Clear of Blows.
	KNIVES	Cutting, Shaping, Gauging, Etc.		Blades Are Very Sharp. . .Hold Knife Very Firmly.
	MAGNIFYING GLASS	Viewing Small Parts to Enable Easier Working.		Never Rest Anything on Glass.
	NEEDLE NOSE PLIER	Holding, Bending, Pulling, Turning Small Wire and Metal Parts. Inserting and Removing Pins.		Do Not Put Too Much Pressure on Ends.
	PIN VISE	Small Drilling. . . Holds Very Small Bits.		When Not in Drill. . . Treat Delicately.
	PLANE	Smoothing Long Surfaces, Thinning Wood Strips.		When Not In Use, Withdraw Blade. Rest Plane on Its Side.
	PLIERS	Holding, Bending, Pulling, Turning Heavy Wire and Other Parts.		See That Jaws Seat Properly and Don't Wobble.
	POWER TOOL	Cuts, Grinds, Shapes, Drills, Sands		Be Sure to Turn It OFF –– Before Putting It Down.
	RAZOR SAW	Cutting Wood Blocks, Masts, Spars, Strips, Etc.		Saw Blade Is Very Sharp. . .Keep Fingers Away.

TOOLS

ILLUSTRATION	NAME	FUNCTION		CAUTION
	SANDER	Smoothing Rough Surfaces		Watch Fingers When Sanding Rapidly.
	SCALE	Measuring Lengths of Any Part		Do Not Bend or Twist Scale.
	SCISSORS	Trimming Lines of Rigging And Cutting Very Thin Material.		Do Not Cut Metal, or Twist, Bend or Pry with It.
	SCREWDRIVER	Setting Screws		Small Screwdrivers Damage Easily. Use Care.
	SCRIBER	An Awl for Marking Lines on Material and Punching Holes.		Hold Scriber Firmly When Pressing into Material.
	SOLDERING IRON	To Solder Small Metal Pieces Together.		Iron Gets Very Hot. . . Always Rest It on Stand.
	TWEEZERS	Holding Small Delicate Pieces While Working.		Edges Are Sharp. Be Careful.
	VISE	Holding Objects While They Are Being Cut, Drilled, Smoothed or Bent.		Do Not Tighten Too Tightly. Do Not Hammer on It.
	WIRECUTTER	Cutting Wires and Thin Material.		Be Careful of Flying Bits of Wire.

INDEX

(Numerals in italics indicate an illustration of the topic mentioned)